EXPLORING
CAREERS

Careers in Emergency Response

Christine Wilcox

ReferencePoint
Press®

© 2017 ReferencePoint Press, Inc.
Printed in the United States

For more information, contact:
ReferencePoint Press, Inc.
PO Box 27779
San Diego, CA 92198
www.ReferencePointPress.com

Picture Credits:
 6: Maury Aaseng
27: Associated Press
35: Gerardo Mora/Newscom
42: Associated Press
52: John Gibbins/Zuma Press/Newscom

LIBRARY OF CONGRESS CATALOGING-IN-PUBLICATION DATA

Names: Wilcox, Christine, author.
Title: Careers in emergency response / by Christine Wilcox.
Description: San Diego, CA : ReferencePoint Press, Inc., 2017. | Series: Exploring careers | Includes
   bibliographical references and index.
Identifiers: LCCN 2016036575 (print) | LCCN 2016044757 (ebook) | ISBN 9781682821046
   (hardback) | ISBN 9781682821053 (eBook)
Subjects: LCSH: Emergency management--Vocational guidance--Juvenile literature. |
   Emergency medical services--Vocational guidance--Juvenile literature. | First responders--
   Juvenile literature.
Classification: LCC HV551.2 .W545 2017 (print) | LCC HV551.2 (ebook) | DDC 363.34/8023--dc23
LC record available at https://lccn.loc.gov/2016036575

Contents

Emergency Response: A Career of Service and Sacrifice

In the United States and around the world, emergency situations—both large and small—are occurring more frequently. According to a report from the *New England Journal of Medicine*, there were three times as many natural disasters between 2000 and 2009 as there were between 1980 and 1989. Scientists predict that climate change will cause even more floods, storms, and wildfires in coming decades, which will be made all the more deadly by a general increase in the population. Mass shootings and terrorist attacks are also on the rise, as is the number of traumatic injuries treated in emergency rooms and trauma centers. In short, there has never been a greater need for emergency response professionals.

What Is Emergency Response?

Emergency response takes many forms. In large-scale disasters, it is called response and recovery (*recovery* refers to actions that occur after a disaster, such as restoring power or cleaning up debris). The federal organization responsible for response and recovery is the Federal Emergency Management Agency (FEMA). During disasters, FEMA mobilizes thousands of professional and volunteer emergency first responders. Emergency response in the medical field is called emergency medical services (EMS). EMS professionals are part of every disaster relief effort, but they also staff ambulances and emergency rooms. Firefighters also spend most of their time providing EMS. Finally, search and rescue (SAR) responders specialize in finding those who are lost, who are buried under debris, or who need to be rescued from dangerous areas.

Not for Everyone

Because compensation varies widely in this profession—from nominal reimbursement provided to SAR specialists to six-figure salaries earned by trauma surgeons—many emergency response professionals will say that there are much easier ways to earn a living. However, these professions have other attractions. First and foremost, these specialists are driven to serve: to help others on what is often the worst day of their lives. Almost all start out as volunteers, and most invest large amounts of time and money pursing training and certifications. Those who have the personality and emotional makeup to stay in this profession consider it to be much more than a job. Emergency response is a calling, and those who work in this field find their jobs extremely rewarding and satisfying.

Careers in emergency response tend to be extremely stressful, at least for short periods of time. Those who gravitate to these jobs thrive under pressure, and they can keep their heads and perform well in chaotic situations. Some of these careers—such as firefighting and search and rescue—thankfully do not get calls to action every day, so those who want nonstop excitement can quickly become disenchanted by the daily chores and duties that go along with the job. Other careers—in particular emergency dispatching and trauma surgery—deal with emergencies on a regular basis. These professionals often experience what is known as occupational burnout. They become emotionally and physically drained, lose their motivation to perform well, become cynical or unfeeling, and ultimately leave their profession. Mental disorders such as depression and post-traumatic stress disorder are also common among emergency responders. Emergency response jobs may seem glamorous, but those who enter these professions must recognize the realities. In short, this is not a career track for everyone.

The Occupational Hazards of Emergency Response

People who work in emergency response describe their jobs as extremely satisfying, but their work can also be dangerous. According to the US Department of Labor, first responders experience more work-related injuries and deaths than most other occupations. And among first responders, job-related injuries are highest among police, sheriff's patrol officers, and firefighters. These graphs show which events are most often associated with injuries for these three groups.

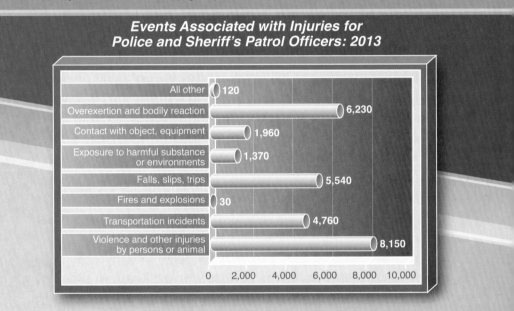

Events Associated with Injuries for Police and Sheriff's Patrol Officers: 2013

- All other: 120
- Overexertion and bodily reaction: 6,230
- Contact with object, equipment: 1,960
- Exposure to harmful substance or environments: 1,370
- Falls, slips, trips: 5,540
- Fires and explosions: 30
- Transportation incidents: 4,760
- Violence and other injuries by persons or animal: 8,150

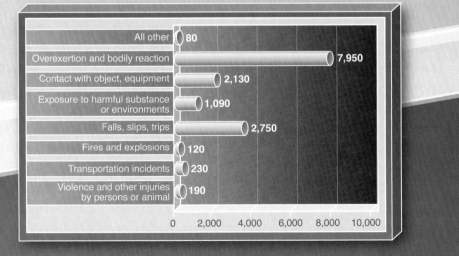

Events Associated with Injuries for Firefighters: 2013

- All other: 80
- Overexertion and bodily reaction: 7,950
- Contact with object, equipment: 2,130
- Exposure to harmful substance or environments: 1,090
- Falls, slips, trips: 2,750
- Fires and explosions: 120
- Transportation incidents: 230
- Violence and other injuries by persons or animal: 190

Source: US Department of Labor, "Characteristics of Individuals and Employment Among First Responders," August 6, 2015.

A Multitude of Skills

All sorts of people are drawn to emergency response professions, so their expertise varies widely. Almost any personal interest or skill set can come into play in emergency response. People who love recreational activities can become lifeguards or join the ski patrol, and hikers and rock climbers can get involved with wilderness and mountain search and rescue. Engineers can help rescuers navigate through partially collapsed structures safely, and chemists can specialize in keeping people safe during a toxic spill or other environmental disaster. Those interested in military careers can join the US Coast Guard, become pararescue specialists (specialists who rescue soldiers trapped behind enemy lines), or emergency medics. Animal trainers can train search and rescue dogs. Pilots can conduct air searches or work in emergency medical transport. Even those who love jumping out of airplanes can become smoke jumpers and rescue people trapped by wildfires.

Because emergency response encompasses so many skills and interests, teens can get involved while they are still in high school. Those interested in emergency medicine can volunteer at their local fire station, emergency services building, or hospital, and they can get certified in first aid and cardiopulmonary resuscitation (CPR). Those interested in search and rescue can join their local SAR group. Volunteering makes a difference, and some teens save lives. For instance, seventeen-year-old lifeguard Harry Higate-Royce saved a nine-year-old boy off a beach in Kent, England. According to a July 2016 article by Mark Duell in the British newspaper the *Daily Mail,* the boy drifted out to sea on an inflatable raft. When Higate-Royce took a rescue board out to the boy to check on him, he discovered the boy could not swim and was too tired to make it back to shore alone. "Because of the direction of the wind, the boy would have eventually been blown towards the chalk reef just north of the bay," explains Higate-Royce's supervisor, crediting the teen with preventing a possibly life-threatening situation.

Giving Back

Emergency response offers a multitude of exciting and rewarding career options. These untraditional careers demand a great deal from those who pursue them, but the brave and committed individuals who step forward to help in an emergency are providing a much-needed service to society. Best of all, they have the satisfaction of knowing that what they do every day makes a difference. Emergency responders are true heroes, to whom many owe their lives.

Emergency Dispatcher

What Does an Emergency Dispatcher Do?

As an emergency dispatcher, Bill Troskey takes over one hundred calls a day in Calhoun County, Michigan. "We deal with a lot of people and in most cases it's the worst day of their lives," Troskey tells Corinne Kellogg of the *Advisor-Chronicle* of Marshall, Michigan. Emergency dispatchers like Troskey are often the first people whom the victims or witnesses of violent or life-threatening emergencies speak with. It is the dispatcher's job to keep these individuals calm and safe while sending them the help they need. The job is stressful—some experts have said it is even more stressful than being an air traffic controller—but Troskey finds it extremely rewarding. "I like being able to help people," he explains in the April 2011 article, "and this job allows me to do that on a pretty continuous basis."

Emergency dispatchers (also known as 911 dispatchers) do far more than just receive emergency calls. They must prioritize those calls based on the nature of the emergency, provide instructions to the caller in what might be a life-and-death situation, and dispatch emergency

At a Glance:
Emergency Dispatcher

Minimum Educational Requirements
High school diploma or equivalent

Personal Qualities
Excellent communication skills; high stress tolerance

Certification
Required in most states

Working Conditions
Indoors

Salary Range
About $24,270 to $59,770

Number of Jobs
As of 2014 about 102,000

Future Job Outlook
Decline of 3 percent through 2024

personnel to the scene. Callers are often panicked or extremely emotional, and the dispatcher must not add to that panic by becoming emotional as well. Instead, he or she must keep the caller calm so that all pertinent information can be gathered and passed along to emergency services. Dispatchers usually have specialized training in handling and soothing distressed callers.

Many call-center dispatchers usually rotate through various roles during their shifts. Dispatchers who take incoming calls, for example, are responsible for determining if the call is an emergency. Typically, more than half of incoming calls are not emergencies. "People call 911 for pretty much anything," Troskey says. "It can be hard having to switch gears when you are dealing with a child not breathing and then you take the next call and there's a guy complaining about the neighbor's barking dog."

If a call is an emergency, the dispatcher determines whether it is a police, fire department, or medical emergency and begins to gather information from the caller. He or she then alerts the dispatcher who is assigned to that area in the call center, who then contacts the appropriate emergency teams. Call centers use specialized computer programs that guide dispatchers through a set of procedures based on the type of emergency, prompt the dispatcher to ask certain questions, and share information among dispatchers and emergency response teams. Dispatchers are also trained in basic emergency medicine and will instruct the caller on how to administer first aid until emergency medical services (EMS) professionals arrive.

In many cases, people use 911 to report a crime in progress. It is the emergency dispatcher's job to gather as much information from the caller as possible to assist the police in apprehending the criminal or criminals. Emergency dispatcher Cameron West spends a great deal of time talking to police officers. "I update them on information that is pertinent to their situation," West explains in a December 2015 interview with Andy Orin of the website Lifehacker. "For example, [if there is a] fight at a bar, we let the officers know who was involved, how many, what they were wearing, which direction they left in and if they were carrying any weapons."

It is no exaggeration to say that the actions of an emergency dispatcher have an enormous impact on the outcome of an emergency.

This can be the best part of the job, but it can also be the worst. There are times when things go wrong or when a dispatcher simply cannot do enough to help those in need. It can be extremely upsetting when a dispatcher loses contact with a victim or victim's family member during a call. It is also emotionally difficult when a frightened child calls 911 to get help, for example, for an ailing parent. In addition, the call center is rarely notified about the outcome of the emergency calls they take, and it can be frustrating not knowing whether a victim survived or the caller got help in time. These situations take a toll on the emotional well-being of dispatchers, and many become burned out. Some even leave their professions.

On the other hand, people who want their jobs to matter will find this occupation extremely satisfying. As Cindra Dunaway, a 911 dispatcher for the Lee County, Florida, Sheriff's Office, writes in the industry blog *PSC Online,*

> Helping bring a baby into the world that didn't want to wait for mom and dad to get to the hospital, assisting in locating a lost child, helping calm someone who has just been victimized, getting that officer his backup when he can't speak for himself . . . can be the most gratifying moment of your busy day. . . . If you can overcome and adapt, if you can perform on a team and be a forward thinker, if you can prepare for the worst day in and day out, then you just might find yourself in the most rewarding career there is.

How Do You Become an Emergency Dispatcher?

Education and the Hiring Process

Most emergency dispatchers are only required to have a high school diploma, but those who are interested in advancement should consider getting a college degree in emergency management, public safety, or a related field. With or without a college degree, the pre-employment process is extensive and can include multiple interviews, skills tests, background investigations, and medical and psychological evaluations.

If an individual is hired, he or she must complete a comprehensive training program, which includes both classroom and on-the-job training. Trainees study topics such as first aid, telecommunications, domestic violence, hazardous materials, suicide intervention, terrorism, and emergency medical dispatch. The training and certification phase of the job varies from state to state. In some localities, the application, interview, and training process can take a year or more.

Volunteer Work and Internships

Becoming an emergency dispatcher requires extensive training; therefore, there are usually no volunteer or internship opportunities available in call centers. However, it may be helpful to have prior experience dealing with emergencies. Volunteering during natural disasters or in emergency medical settings will also help potential applicants get a sense of whether this job is right for them.

Skills and Personality

According to Jeff Troyer, executive director of the Kalamazoo County Consolidated Dispatch Authority, "Less than 1 percent of the population can actually do this job." Dispatchers must be quick, efficient, and extremely accurate while under extreme stress. The ability to multitask is paramount. As Troyer tells Kellogg of the *Advisor-Chronicle*, "[It is] a position that takes multi-tasking to a whole other level." Regardless of the emergency, dispatchers must be able to relate information to emergency services through a complex computer system while simultaneously instructing and calming a caller. They also must perform their job with the knowledge that mistakes can cost people their lives and that everything they say and do is recorded and may be reviewed by government officials or scrutinized by the media.

The type of personality suited to this job is energized, rather than depleted, by highly stressful situations and gets personal satisfaction from performing well during a crisis. Dispatchers must be confident, comfortable taking charge of dangerous situations, and able to make quick decisions. They also must have superior communication skills and be able to speak courteously to everyone with whom they come in contact—regardless of the situation. It is not uncommon for callers to be angry, or even abusive, when they call 911, and dispatchers must not take this abuse personally.

On the Job

Employers

Emergency dispatchers are almost always government employees—usually on the state or local level. Some localities will hire dispatchers specifically for their police and fire departments, and the dispatchers will work in and be supervised by that department. Private hospitals and security firms also hire emergency dispatchers. These private organizations have their own training and certification requirements.

Working Conditions

Emergency dispatchers work indoors in communication centers, which are sometimes called public safety answering points. Most dispatchers work eight- to twelve-hour shifts, though some employers require longer shifts. Communication centers are open twenty-four hours a day, every day of the year, and dispatchers can expect to work evenings, weekends, and holidays. Dispatchers with more seniority tend to receive more desirable shifts. Overtime is often required.

Earnings

In 2015 the pay range for an emergency dispatcher was $24,270 to $59,770 per year, with a median salary of $38,010, or $18.27 per hour. Salary usually depends on the state or local budget for emergency services, so dispatchers in wealthier localities often make more than those in poorer localities.

Opportunities for Advancement

Emergency dispatchers can move into supervisory positions. However, a 911 supervisor must have more than on-the-job experience;

he or she usually must receive additional training and certification. Training can cover concepts such as management, technical trouble-shooting of the emergency response system, and media relations.

For people interested in moving beyond the role of dispatcher, there are a few other career options. Some dispatchers become 911 trainers, and others focus on quality assurance, policy development, or administrative oversight. Still others become involved in the design of the emergency communication system. These positions usually require a degree in a field such as public administration or emergency management as well as significant amounts of professional experience.

What Is the Future Outlook for Emergency Dispatchers?

As more and more people have access to cell phones, calls to 911 centers have increased. However, the US Bureau of Labor Statistics (BLS) still projects a 3 percent decline in the employment of emergency dispatchers from 2014 to 2024. Some of this decline is technology driven; as 911 systems have become more efficient, emergency communication centers have been able to consolidate and serve larger areas. In addition, there has been a general trend of budget cuts among local and state governments, which employ most emergency dispatchers. For these reasons, fewer dispatchers are expected to be hired in the future.

Even though employment is decreasing, there is always a demand for skilled dispatchers. The reality is that turnover among these professionals is high. An emergency dispatcher's work is stressful and demanding, and it is not uncommon for dispatchers to burn out or to realize that they are not suited for the job. The industry expects a large number of dispatchers to move on to other employment in the coming decade.

The bottom line is that governments are always in need of effective dispatchers. If a person has the right combination of skills and temperament to thrive in this profession, he or she will almost certainly be able to find employment.

Find Out More

Association of Public-Safety Communications Officials (APCO) International
351 N. Williamson Blvd.
Daytona Beach, FL 32114
website: www.apcointl.org

APCO International is the world's largest organization of public safety communications professionals. It provides expertise, professional development, technical assistance, advocacy, and outreach to emergency call centers worldwide. It also offers training and certification programs for emergency dispatchers. Its website contains resources, articles, and links to online publications.

National Emergency Number Association (NENA)
1700 Diagonal Rd., Suite 500
Alexandria, VA 22314
website: www.nena.org

NENA is a professional organization focused on 911 education, operations, policy, and technology. Its website has information about training and education, conferences, membership, and links to articles in its industry magazine, the *Call*.

911DispatcherEDU.org
website: www.911dispatcheredu.org

911DispatcherEDU.org is a website devoted to information for people interested in becoming an emergency dispatcher. The website contains general information about what it is like to be a dispatcher, duties and responsibilities, how to get a job, how to get certified, and salary information. It also has information about 911 dispatcher specializations, including fire, EMS, and police dispatchers.

9-1-1 Magazine
website: www.9-1-1magazine.com

Established in 1989, *9-1-1 Magazine* is an online publication of interest to people in the emergency communications field. Its website contains hundreds of articles, many of which describe day-to-day work as an emergency dispatcher as well as information about training and education.

Emergency Medical Technician

What Does an Emergency Medical Technician Do?

At a Glance:
Emergency Medical Technician

Minimum Educational Requirements
High school diploma or equivalent

Personal Qualities
Excellent interpersonal and critical-thinking skills; physical strength

Certification
Required

Working Conditions
Indoors and outdoors

Salary Range
About $20,860 to $55,110

Number of Jobs
As of 2014 about 241,200

Future Job Outlook
Projected increase of 24 percent through 2024

In an emergency, the first medical professional on the scene is often an emergency medical technician (EMT). EMTs are trained professionals who care for the sick and injured in emergency situations. They treat and stabilize their patients and transport them to a hospital emergency room or other health care facility. When an ambulance arrives at the scene of an emergency, it is staffed by EMTs.

Most people become EMTs because they want to save lives. However, the truth is that most of the calls EMTs receive are not life threatening. "To be honest, it's not like TV, where we save a life every day," explains Nate Dionne, an EMT who works for the business emergency medical services system in South Carolina. As Dionne tells Brett and Kate McKay in an interview with *The Art of Manliness*, a general interest website that sometimes profiles people who have interesting jobs, "The calls where you make a difference between life and death are few and far between." On a typical twenty-four-hour shift, an EMT team may be dispatched to assist an elderly person who has fallen, to transport a patient from a nursing home to a dialysis center, to stand by at a local festival, and to check the victims of a minor automobile accident for injuries. However, when a serious emergency happens, it is the actions of the EMT team that often makes the difference between life and death. It is these moments that make the job so rewarding. As Dionne explains, "When you do [save a life], it's a wonderful feeling. It feels like your whole career is worth that one save."

What EMTs actually do on the job depends on their level of training as well as the laws of the state in which they work. There are three basic levels of EMT training and certification: EMT-basic (also known as EMT-B), EMT-intermediate (also known as advanced EMT), and paramedic. EMTs with basic training are qualified to care for patients and administer first aid at the scene of an accident or during transport to the hospital. They can manage breathing, heart, and trauma emergencies. EMTs with intermediate training can give patients medication, administer intravenous fluids, and deal with more serious emergencies. Paramedics are highly trained health care providers who can interpret complex diagnostic tests such as electrocardiograms (which monitor heart function), give medications, and perform some lifesaving procedures, such as inserting an airway tube down the esophagus of a patient who is not breathing (called intubation). Many people compare paramedics to nurses; although they are trained in different areas, their knowledge and skills are roughly equivalent.

During their shifts (which can be up to forty-eight hours long), EMTs live and work at the emergency services building in which they are stationed. In smaller cities or towns, this is often the fire station (most firefighters are also EMTs). While on duty, EMTs inventory the ambulance and do maintenance on equipment, practice procedures and perform emergency drills, and eat and sleep on-site. When a call comes in from the emergency dispatcher, they respond immediately. At the scene, they assess a patient's condition, consult with an on-call physician as needed, stabilize the patient, and transport him or her to the hospital. When they arrive, they are responsible for accurately and efficiently reporting all information about the patient's condition to health care staff. They must also document all medical care given to patients and all materials used so that the ambulance can be re-stocked. Some EMT teams work on medical transport helicopters or airplanes to transport critically injured people to hospitals. Because only the most injured or ill people are transported by air, paramedics usually staff these positions.

EMTs go through hundreds of hours of training. They work long, erratic hours for relatively low pay. Most EMTs find the job frustrating, boring, extremely stressful, frightening, and exhilarating—sometimes all in the same day. "It can be very hard," explains Dionne. "But it is also the most rewarding job in the world. I cannot imagine doing anything else with my life."

How Do You Become an Emergency Medical Technician?

Education

All states require EMTs to be licensed by the state in which they work. To be issued a license, individuals must complete a certified postsecondary educational program in emergency medical technology and pass a national certification exam given by the National Registry of Emergency Medical Technicians.

To be accepted to an educational program, students typically must have a high school diploma (or the equivalent) and a CPR certification. Programs are offered through technical institutes or community colleges and usually require 100 to 150 hours of instruction for EMT-basic certification. Topics covered in basic coursework include assessing patient condition, dealing with trauma and cardiac emergencies, using field equipment, and driving an ambulance. Advanced EMT training takes considerably longer. Paramedics train for several years and usually receive an associate's degree upon completion of training. Some paramedics say that paramedic training is more difficult and intense than earning a four-year college degree.

After completing training and passing the certification exam, individuals may then apply for licensure in their state. Some states have additional requirements, such as passing a state equivalency exam and a background check.

Volunteer Work and Internships

Many people volunteer as EMTs to help their neighbors and give back to their communities. Communities always need certified EMTs to staff their volunteer shifts; in fact, in some poorer localities, almost all EMTs are volunteers. Volunteer EMTs must receive the same training and pass the same certification tests as paid EMTs, though they usually work shorter hours than paid EMTs. Volunteering as an EMT is an excellent way to prepare for a career in another health care or emergency services field.

EMTs must be eighteen years old to become certified. However, high school students interested in becoming EMTs should ask if their local fire department or emergency services center has a junior EMT program. The goal of these programs is to show young people what it is like to be an EMT and encourage them to become certified once they are eighteen.

Teens who want to become junior EMTs must first complete a junior EMT training program. Each locality has its own requirements, such as maintaining a minimum grade point average, having a clean driving record, and passing a drug screening. The role of a junior EMT depends on state and local laws. Some junior EMTs ride along in ambulances as observers; others help assess patients and provide basic first aid. Junior EMTs also participate in training drills, help maintain the equipment and stock the ambulances, and participate in community outreach programs.

Skills and Personality

Many people want to become EMTs because they enjoy the excitement that comes with responding to emergency situations. However, since most EMT calls are not true emergencies, some technicians become bored or disillusioned with the routine nature of much of the job. The people who get most satisfaction from this work are those who have a strong desire to help others—regardless of what form that takes. The most successful EMTs believe that their purpose is to serve. To these professionals, reassuring a confused and frightened elderly person in the middle of the night is just as meaningful as pulling an accident victim from a car wreck.

Working as an EMT can also be extremely stressful. Technicians must remain calm even during life-and-death emergencies. They must also be careful, active listeners. According to a November 2011 article on the EMS1 website, an online resource for emergency medical services (EMS) workers, "It's important to speak to [patients] . . . calmly and with confidence and even more important to listen to what they're saying. If you're distracted and not really listening, you can miss crucial information."

EMTs must also be excellent problem solvers who can employ deductive reasoning when diagnosing patients. They also need physical strength and mental stamina and must not be squeamish about blood and bodily fluids.

On the Job

Employers

EMTs and paramedics are employed by state, local, and private hospitals; state and local governments; and privately owned and operated ambulance services. Often, private EMS companies are contracted to take nonemergency calls, such as transporting chronically ill patients to medical appointments. However, it is becoming more and more common for these private companies to handle all of a locality's 911 and EMS needs.

Working Conditions

EMTs typically work twelve- to twenty-four-hour shifts at the hospital, fire station, or EMS center. Shifts can fall on evenings, weekends, and holidays. Most paid EMTs work full time, and many work more than forty hours a week.

When out on an emergency call, EMTs are required to bend and kneel, carry heavy equipment, and lift patients onto stretchers. They sometimes must put themselves in dangerous situations; an EMT may have to crawl into a wrecked automobile or a partially collapsed building to reach a victim. EMTs can also be exposed to infectious diseases and can be injured by patients who are violent.

Earnings

In 2015 the pay range for an EMT was $20,860 to $55,110 per year, with a median salary of $31,980, or $15.38 per hour. EMTs with basic certification earn the lowest salary; paramedics earn the highest. Hospitals tend to offer the most competitive pay, and private ambulance services tend to offer the lowest pay. EMTs working for state or local governments in wealthier localities may make more than those working in poorer localities.

Opportunities for Advancement

Many people become EMTs as a way to gain invaluable medical experience before entering other careers in health care or emergency services. Most firefighters are also EMTs, and many physician assistants, nurses, and doctors once worked as EMTs. Career EMTs usually become paramedics. Experienced paramedics can also advance within the rank structure of their organization and become supervisors, managers, or instructors.

What Is the Future Outlook for Emergency Medical Technicians?

The increase in the elderly population will drive an increase in the need for EMTs over the next decade. The US Bureau of Labor Statistics (BLS) projects a 24 percent increase in the employment of EMTs from 2014 to 2024, a growth rate that is much faster than average. As the aging population increases, there will be more age-related emergencies, such as heart attacks, strokes, and falls. There will also be more specialized medical facilities that treat older people, such as dialysis centers, and more EMTs will be needed to transport patients from hospitals and nursing homes to these facilities.

There is high turnover in the EMT field. Because shifts are long and pay can be low, many people seek other employment once they get older or have a family. Others only intend to work as EMTs for a short time and then move on to other careers. This high rate of turnover, coupled with the projected increase in employment, means that certified EMTs and paramedics should have no problem finding employment in the years to come.

Find Out More

EMS Daily News
website: www.emsdailynews.com

EMS Daily News is an online news source that rounds up national and international news stories, articles, and blog posts related to EMS. Its website has an extensive library of articles that will give those interested in becoming an EMT or paramedic information about the ways EMS professionals work within their communities.

EMS.gov
National Highway Traffic Safety Administration
Office of Emergency Medical Services
1200 New Jersey Ave. SE
Washington, DC 20590
website: www.ems.gov

EMS.gov is the website of the National Highway Traffic Safety Administration's Office of EMS, which supports national EMS systems, projects, and research. The website contains data and statistics, reports about EMS, webinars, and the newsletter *EMS Update.*

EMS1
website: www.ems1.com

EMS1 is a clearinghouse for news, education, and job opportunities for EMTs and other EMS professionals. Its website includes articles, newsletters, and videos about EMS as well as detailed information for those considering a career in EMS.

National Association of Emergency Medical Technicians (NAEMT)
PO Box 1400
Clinton, MS 39060
website: www.naemt.org

The NAEMT is a nonprofit organization that supports and educates EMTs, paramedics, first responders, and other professionals working in prehospital emergency medicine. Its website includes descriptions of its various education programs and has detailed information about how to pursue a career in EMS.

Paramedic.com
website: www.paramedic.com

Paramedic.com is the division of EMS1 that focuses on information specific to paramedics. The website features the MedicCast podcast, which discusses medical care, emergency procedures, and day-to-day advice for EMS professionals. It also features ParamedicTV, a series of videos featuring medical and emergency techniques and other topics related to careers in paramedicine.

Firefighter

What Does a Firefighter Do?

Firefighting is an exciting and highly rewarding career—one that many young people dream of pursuing. "I think that at some point in their life boys want to be firefighters," explains Captain Michael Baker, a firefighter for the Tulsa Fire Department in Oklahoma. As he tells Brett and Kate McKay in an October 2008 interview for *The Art of Manliness* blog, "The thrill of the red lights, siren, and hero factor all plays into the desire." Of course, girls also dream of becoming firefighters, as do plenty of adults. It is a career that sounds appealing to anyone who is drawn to the idea of heroically risking his or her life to save others.

However, people who become firefighters because they think they will spend most of their time facing danger and saving lives are usually disappointed by their career choice. At the typical fire station, most of the calls are not life-and-death emergencies, and many firefighters go their whole careers without ever saving a life. Firefighting is not just about

At a Glance:
Firefighter

Minimum Educational Requirements
High school diploma or equivalent

Personal Qualities
Excellent interpersonal and problem-solving skills; bravery; physical strength

Specialized Training
Required

Working Conditions
Indoors and outdoors; high risk of injury

Salary Range
About $23,010 to $79,490

Number of Jobs
As of 2014 about 327,300

Future Job Outlook
Growth rate of 5 percent through 2024

handling emergencies; it is about helping others. This can mean driving an elderly person to a doctor's appointment, standing by at a festival in case someone gets hurt, performing fire inspections on new buildings, or even assisting a person who is under the influence of drugs or alcohol. As Baker explains, "Deep down, firefighters are born with a desire to serve the community." Those who succeed in this career understand that a life of service can be frustrating at times, but they also derive great satisfaction from serving others and knowing that they can handle any emergency, big or small.

When there is a fire, firefighters use specialized equipment to enter buildings; rescue and render medical assistance to those trapped inside; put out the fire using water hoses, fire extinguishers, and water pumps; secure the area; and search the debris to help determine the fire's cause. This work is extremely hazardous—fires are unpredictable, emit deadly gasses, and make structures highly unstable. During the terrorist attack in New York City on September 11, 2001, 343 firefighters and paramedics lost their lives when the World Trade Center's twin towers collapsed. Many of these men and women were volunteer or off-duty firefighters who rushed to the scene when they learned of the attacks. Many more civilians would have lost their lives were it not for their sacrifice.

Firefighters do much more than put out fires and rescue people from burning buildings. They respond to all types of emergencies, from automobile accidents to natural disasters. Some firefighters specialize in working with hazardous materials like chemicals or crude oil. Wildland firefighters are specially trained to control forest fires. They prevent these fires from reaching populated areas by cutting down trees in a line around a fire to contain it. Other firefighters are trained to investigate the cause of fires and determine if they are accidental or the result of arson. All firefighters have medical training, and most are also emergency medical technicians (EMTs) or paramedics. According to the National Fire Protection Association, two out of three calls to firefighters are medical emergencies, and at some stations almost all calls are medical in nature.

When not on emergency calls, firefighters live, eat, and sleep at the fire station during their shifts, which are usually twenty-four to forty-eight hours long. While on duty, firefighters must maintain the emergency vehicles, keep all necessary records, and do the routine chores necessary to keep the station clean and running smoothly. Nonemergency work includes training and continuing education, educating the public, and performing fire inspections in the community. Firefighters also supervise and educate volunteers and new employees.

How Do You Become a Firefighter?

Education and the Hiring Process

Firefighting is one of the most difficult emergency services careers to break into. Because it is such a desirable profession, competition for jobs is fierce. Most departments will receive hundreds of applications for a single position, and the hiring process can take six months or more.

Young people who want to become firefighters should start to prepare while they are in high school. Good grades, a clean driving record, a high level of physical fitness, and good employer references are all important, as is demonstrating a commitment to community service through volunteer work. It can also be helpful to learn a second language if there is a significant non-English-speaking minority population in the community.

Teens should also find out what is involved in the hiring process in their locality as early as possible. There is usually an entry-level test that applicants must take to be considered for an open position, and some experts suggest that students take the test in high school for practice. In many localities, the test is only given once every year or two, and if an applicant does not pass, he or she will not have another opportunity to retake the test during that hiring cycle. Most departments also require their firefighters to have CPR and basic EMT certification before they are hired, and some even require that their new hires are already advanced EMTs or paramedics with a few years of experience under their belts. In addition, it may be helpful to earn a fire technology certificate from a local community college (some localities require all paid and volunteer firefighters to be certified). At minimum, applicants must be at least eighteen years old with a high

A firefighter sprays water on a wildfire that threatens people and property. Firefighters put out fires and rescue people from burning buildings and other types of fires, and also respond to emergencies including car accidents and natural disasters.

school diploma and a valid driver's license. They must pass a medical exam, a drug screening test, and a detailed background check. It can take some time to gather the information necessary for the background check, so applicants should start that process early.

After being hired, firefighters must attend an in-depth training program at a local or state fire academy. This training can last several months. Firefighters must then go through a probationary period or apprenticeship while they learn the skills and procedures specific to their fire department. Training and education is usually ongoing for working firefighters, especially those who are seeking promotion. To advance to higher ranks within a fire department, a college degree is often required.

Volunteer Work and Internships

Almost all career firefighters start out as either volunteer firefighters or volunteer or paid EMTs. According to the US Bureau of Labor Statistics (BLS), there are twice as many volunteer firefighters as there are paid firefighters working in the United States. And according to the National Fire Protection Association, about 69 percent of fire departments were staffed entirely by volunteer firefighters in 2013.

Many departments have cadet volunteer programs that allow high school students to get a sense of whether or not they want to pursue firefighting as a career. Students can also volunteer for wildland firefighting crews during the summer months, and those with EMT certifications may be able to volunteer in hospital emergency rooms.

Skills and Personality

Some young people who want to be firefighters imagine that they will put their own lives at risk to save others on a regular basis. According to Steve Prziborowski, a career firefighter who writes a column for the website, FireRescue1, this is a mistaken notion and not the reason to become a firefighter. "If you're getting into this line of work to fight fire and save lives, you're going to be disappointed and possibly unhappy with your choice of occupation," he writes in an April 2015 article. "I have seen it happen when firefighters with a year or two on the job say how unhappy they are because their department doesn't fight that much fire and because they have yet to save anyone's life." For this reason, people who crave constant excitement will probably not be satisfied with this career.

The most successful firefighters want to help others more than they want to be heroes. They are calm in a crisis, can make quick decisions under pressure, and can do their jobs regardless of what is going on around them. They have excellent communication skills and can take charge in situations where people are injured or frightened. And because they must work in dangerous—and sometimes life-threatening—situations, they must be courageous.

In addition, firefighters must have a certain degree of physical strength and stamina. They must also work well as members of a team.

On the Job

Employers

According to the BLS, about 90 percent of firefighters work for local governments, and most of the remainder work for federal and state governments. Career firefighters can also work at airports, industrial sites, or chemical plants.

Working Conditions

Of all occupations, being a firefighter has one of the highest rates of illness and injury. Building collapse, smoke inhalation, falls, vehicle explosions, and overexposure to heat and flames are all potential risks. Protective gear can be heavy, hot, and uncomfortable. In addition, firefighters must help people who are under extreme stress, who sometimes become violent. There is also a risk of contracting diseases from sick or injured patients.

When not on call, firefighters spend most of their working hours at the fire station. Shifts are usually twenty-four to forty-eight hours long, followed by several days off, though this varies from department to department. Most work weekends and holidays, and during emergencies they will work extended hours. Wildland firefighters can battle a forest fire for weeks at a time. Many firefighters work more than forty hours a week.

One thing that most firefighters enjoy about the job is the camaraderie that forms between coworkers. Living and working together toward a common purpose creates strong bonds among firefighters.

Earnings

In 2015 the pay range for firefighters was $23,010 to $79,490 per year, with a median salary of $46,870, or $22.53 per hour. Firefighting is one of the few professional occupations in which people without a college degree can earn a living wage and have job security for their entire careers. Most firefighters belong to a union, which helps to protect their jobs and negotiate good pay rates and retirement packages. The largest firefighter union is the International Association of Fire Fighters.

Opportunities for Advancement

The rank structure among firefighters is similar to the rank structure in the military. According to the BLS, firefighters can be promoted to engineer, lieutenant, captain, battalion chief, assistant chief, deputy chief, and chief. Advanced education and testing is required at each stage of promotion, and some departments require those in the higher ranks to have bachelor's degrees.

Some firefighters go on to have careers in law enforcement as fire investigators, and some move on to related careers in science and engineering.

What Is the Future Outlook for Firefighters?

According to the BLS, firefighting as an industry is growing at an average rate of about 5 percent. However, many localities are facing budget cuts and are relying more and more on volunteer firefighters to staff their departments. And because becoming a firefighter is such a desirable occupation, there is very little turnover. For these reasons, this field will remain extremely competitive for the foreseeable future.

Find Out More

FireRescue1
website: www.firerescue1.com

FireRescue1 is an online resource for firefighters. Its website contains information about careers in firefighting, including videos, job lists, news articles, and blog posts about how to become a firefighter.

FireScience.org
website: www.firescience.org

FireScience.org has detailed information about how to pursue a career in fire science, firefighting, or a related public service career. Its website contains up-to-date information about developments in the field of fire science, evaluations of educational programs, and scholarship information.

International Association of Women in Fire & Emergency Service (iWomen)
1707 Ibis Dr.
Buffalo, MN 55313
website: www.i-women.org

iWomen is an organization that supports women firefighters and first responders. It works to address women's issues in the profession and provides education, support, and advocacy for female firefighters. Its website contains articles and resources related to women in first responder professions as well as links to related websites.

National Fire Protection Association (NFPA)
1 Batterymarch Pk.
Quincy, MA 02169
website: www.nfpa.org

The NFPA is a nonprofit organization devoted to educating and training firefighting processionals and the public about fire safety. Its website contains information about fire safety and firefighting as well as links to multiple blogs, newsletters, and other publications of interest to firefighters.

US Fire Administration (USFA)
16825 S. Seton Ave.
Emmitsburg, MD 21727
website: www.usfa.fema.gov

The USFA is part of the Federal Emergency Management Agency and the US Department of Homeland Security. It works to support firefighting organizations in preventing and responding to fire emergencies and runs the National Fire Academy. Its website contains information about training and professional development for firefighters, statistics pertaining to firefighting, and a link to a national library with hundreds of thousands of resources about fire technology and prevention.

Police Officer

What Does a Police Officer Do?

On June 12, 2016, gunman Omar Mateen opened fire inside the Pulse nightclub in Orlando, Florida, killing forty-nine people and injuring fifty-three others. Police officers entered the building a few minutes after the first shots were fired. In the chaos, officers evacuated patrons, carried out the wounded, and secured areas of the club. They reentered the club again and again, protecting patrons from the shooter until the special weapons and tactics (SWAT) team arrived.

The patrol officers who responded acted heroically while putting themselves in grave danger. Once such officer was Luke Austin, who evacuated a wounded man in the middle of an exchange of gunfire between Mateen and SWAT officers. Once the shooting victim was brought outside, Austin comforted him. "I remained on my hands and knees looking into the victim's eyes while talking to him to 'Stay with me, I am here with you, your [sic] safe now,'" Austin wrote in the police report detailing the incident, portions of which were published in

At a Glance:
Police Officer

Minimum Educational Requirements
High school diploma; some localities require a bachelor's degree

Personal Qualities
Excellent interpersonal skills; bravery; strength and stamina

Specialized Training
Required

Working Conditions
Indoors and outdoors; high risk of injury

Salary Range
About $34,170 to $112,200

Number of Jobs
As of 2014 about 806,400

Future Job Outlook
Growth rate of 4 percent through 2024

a July 2016 article by Gal Tziperman Lotan for the *Orlando Sentinel*. He brought the injured man to the local fire station and then rushed back to the club to rescue more victims.

A police officer's role is to maintain law and order and protect citizens and property. Much of their day is spent in a station house, patrolling, or performing other routine public safety tasks, but quite often they are called upon to deal with emergency situations. Patrol officers (police who enforce the law within a specific community) are often the first on the scene of dangerous situations such as the Orlando shooting. At a vehicle accident, police provide emergency rescue and medical care until emergency medical services (EMS) personnel arrive. They respond to crimes in progress, such as fights, muggings, and home invasions. They assist EMS with patients who may be dangerous or mentally unstable. In all their functions, they get to know the citizens and the layout of their community so that they can respond efficiently and effectively to large-scale emergencies.

When responding to disasters, police officers have two main roles: to be first responders (a term that means a person has been trained to provide medical care to an individual until emergency medical services can arrive on the scene) and to provide for the security and safety of the public. Because police departments are typically the public organization that is most familiar with the affected community, they play a big role in coordinating emergency responses. For instance, when Hurricane Sandy hit the east coast of the United States in 2012, police in affected communities went house to house to help people who were trapped, injured, or in need. One such resident in Bridgewater, New Jersey, was an organ transplant survivor suffering from pneumonia whose generator was very low on fuel; because the local police department reached out to their residents, they were aware of the person's situation and were able to help. Local police departments also directed and manned rescue boats, provided emergency first aid, closed roadways and redirect traffic, and maintained security in unsafe areas.

Some police departments have specialized emergency response teams to respond to difficult or high-risk law enforcement situations. These teams are known as SWAT teams or emergency response teams. Members are trained in advanced weaponry and specialized skills. While these teams are usually not called out in natural disasters, they do respond to emergency situations where suspects have barricaded themselves in a building, have taken hostages, or are otherwise placing others at risk. These teams are trained in methods that resolve dangerous situations as safely as possible, and they have been found to reduce the risk of injury or loss of life to police officers, suspects, and innocent bystanders.

Police departments in large, metropolitan areas such as New York City often have emergency service units (ESUs). Members of ESUs are trained in SWAT, but they also respond in a variety of other emergency situations. Depending on where they are located, they may have specialized training in hazardous material incidents, in rescue and evacuation in unstable structures or building collapses, in surface or underwater rescue, in fire suppression and rescue, and in search and evidence recovery after a disaster.

How Do You Become a Police Officer?

Education and the Hiring Process

Police officers are required to have a high school diploma or the equivalent, though in some agencies a bachelor's degree is required. The hiring process for police officers is time consuming and extensive, and students interested in becoming police officers should find out what the process entails as early as possible. To be considered, a candidate usually must be twenty-one years old, a US citizen, and pass a rigorous background check. (A felony or a drug conviction may disqualify a person from becoming a police officer.) A candidate must also be in good physical and mental health and pass a physical fitness test and an extensive medical exam. There is also a written entrance exam and an oral board review, which is an in-depth interview conducted by three or more people (which can include police officers, officials, and members of the community). Strong performance in this interview is crucial to getting hired. The board asks questions designed to reveal how an applicant will behave on the job. It looks for strong communication skills and an ability to quickly evaluate a situation and make good decisions under pressure.

In most localities, candidates must also attend a law enforcement training academy before working as a police officer. In some cases, a candidate is hired and then sent to a police academy at the cost of the department. In other cases, candidates must complete academy training at their own expense before being hired. Police academy programs typically take six to eight months to complete. Requirements

A police officer carries a child who was rescued during a hurricane. Police officers respond to accidents, emergencies, and crimes in progress. During routine patrols, their presence often serves as a deterrent to crime.

are determined by law and vary from state to state. While at the academy, candidates study topics such as constitutional and state law, safe firearm and driving techniques, how to apprehend a criminal, how to relate to the community, and how to respond to emergency situations. Police officers are also required to be trained as first responders and must know how to respond to medical and other emergencies. After being hired, most departments require a period of on-the-job training, and many encourage officers to take additional educational courses.

Police interested in working on SWAT teams or ESUs typically have a bachelor's degree in criminal justice or law enforcement and at least five years of experience as a patrol officer. Once assigned to the team, they receive specialized training in areas such as firearms and specialized equipment, self-defense, crisis intervention, and crowd control.

Volunteer Work and Internships

Some police departments offer cadet programs to interested candidates who are younger than that department's hiring age or who are still attending high school or college. Cadets work within departments doing clerical work and gaining experience in law enforcement that can help them get a job later. These unpaid volunteer or internship programs go under many names and are offered by most larger police departments.

Skills and Personality

Police officers must have physical strength and stamina, good judgment, and excellent communication skills. They must also be able to take charge in stressful or dangerous situations and be comfortable being a highly visible member of their communities. Perceptiveness is also an important quality; police officers must be able to understand and anticipate the reactions of those with whom they interact.

Police officers must also be able to control their emotions in stressful situations. According to Larry Capps, retired assistant chief of the Missouri City, Texas, police department, self-control, self-discipline, and emotional maturity are all crucial attributes of a good police officer. "When police officers encounter citizens who lose their temper, resolving the contact becomes more difficult," he writes in a December 2014 article for the *FBI Law Enforcement Bulletin*. "If officers respond by losing their own temper, the circumstances become incendiary and often lead to a less-than-desirable result for both parties."

In addition to these traits, members of ESUs must know how to work effectively as a team. They must also be willing to put themselves in dangerous situations on a regular basis and be able to do their jobs under great stress.

Employers

Police are employed by the government—they work for local or state police departments or for federal law enforcement organizations. Federal law enforcement organizations in the United States include the Federal Bureau of Investigation (FBI), the US Marshals Service, the Drug Enforcement Administration, and the Bureau of Alcohol, Tobacco, Firearms, and Explosives.

Working Conditions

Police work can be stressful and physically demanding. Patrol officers spend most of their shifts away from the station and may be required to subdue suspects or pursue them on foot. Some police officers work in administrative positions and spend their days indoors.

Police work can also be dangerous. Patrol officers have one of the highest rates of illness or injury of all occupations. They are most often injured by vehicles, but they are also injured in conflicts with criminals and during emergency situations. In addition, they risk exposure to disease from victims or suspects with whom they come in contact.

Most police officers work full-time, and overtime is common. Many police officers are required to work evening, weekend, or holiday shifts.

Earnings

According to the US Bureau of Labor Statistics (BLS), in 2015 the pay range for law enforcement officers was $34,170 to $100,560 per year, with a median salary of $60,270, or $28.97 per hour. Patrol officers earned a median salary of $58,320 per year. Members of SWAT teams or other emergency response teams will earn a higher-than-average salary. The FBI reports that SWAT team agents within the FBI earn an average salary of $74,800 to $112,200.

Opportunities for Advancement

The rank structure in law enforcement is similar to the rank structure in the military. Promotions within the police force are based on job and testing performance and come with standardized pay raises. Officers can be promoted to supervisory positions (sergeant, captain, etc.) or to investigative positions (detective). For promotion to or within emergency response units, advanced training and education is required.

What Is the Future Outlook for Police Officers?

Employment of police officers is projected to grow at a rate of about 4 percent, slightly slower than average. Crime rates have fallen overall in recent years, and many localities face budget cuts. However, the number of job opportunities for police officers varies year to year based on changes in budgets and in the needs of a given community. According to the BLS, applicants who have a college degree or military experience and who speak a second language have a good chance of being hired as a police officer. Also, because of the increase in terrorist activities, mass shootings, and natural disasters, many police departments are forming emergency response units or strengthening the units they already have in place.

Find Out More

American Special Ops
website: www.americanspecialops.com

American Special Ops is a website devoted to special operations law enforcement careers available in the United States, including SWAT; the FBI Hostage Rescue Team; and military emergency response units like

Rangers (army), SEALs (navy), and pararescuemen (air force). The website includes eligibility requirements for specific emergency response careers, videos, details about past missions, and other information relevant to those seeking emergency response careers in law enforcement.

Criminal Justice USA
website: www.criminaljusticeusa.com

Criminal Justice USA is an information website that provides aspiring criminal justice students and professionals with resources and information on law enforcement careers. The website contains information about how to start a career in law enforcement and degree programs available by state as well as a blog addressing topics of interest to law enforcement.

Fraternal Order of Police (FOP)
701 Marriott Dr.
Nashville, TN 37214
website: www.fop.net

FOP is the largest organization in support of police officers in the United States. It works to improve the safety of police officers through education, legislation, and community involvement. Its website includes training webinars, jobs listings, articles, and general information about careers in law enforcement of interest to students interested in emergency police work.

GoLawEnforcement
website: www.golawenforcement.com

GoLawEnforcment is a website aimed at people interested in a career in law enforcement. The site discusses various career paths and roles, explains various education options, includes study guides that can help applicants pass examinations, and details the hiring process.

PoliceOne
website: www.policeone.com

PoliceOne is a website devoted to providing information and resources to law enforcement officers, including those specializing in emergency response. The website includes several sections dealing with emergency response and preparedness, including articles, resource links, videos, and career information, including job postings.

Emergency Nurse

At the University of Texas Medical Branch (UTMB) emergency room (ER) in Galveston, Texas, emergency nurse Kelly Ferguson is assigned to cover several of the ER's exam rooms. In less than an hour, she questions a young man who has lung cancer and is complaining of shortness of breath; treats a convict with elevated blood pressure who has been brought from the local prison (he later escapes); assesses an elderly patient who is showing signs of a possible stroke in progress; checks in six patients; and completes three blood draws, three blood pressure readings, and six chart notes. "It's unusually slow today," she explained to India Ogazi, who was shadowing her for a January 2015 article for the *UTMB Health Impact* newsletter.

Emergency nursing is fast paced, chaotic, and exhausting, but most of the nurses who staff emergency rooms and trauma units say that it is also extremely rewarding. Ferguson, who has a passion for helping others in need, fell in love with emergency nursing after being assigned to

At a Glance:
Emergency Nurse

Minimum Educational Requirements
Bachelor's or associate's degree in nursing or completion of approved nursing program

Personal Qualities
Excellent interpersonal and critical-thinking skills; calm under stress; compassion

Certification
Optional

Working Conditions
Indoors

Salary Range
About $46,360 to $171,560

Number of Jobs
As of 2014 about 2,751,000

Future Job Outlook
Growth rate of 26 percent through 2024

the ER while completing her nursing degree at UTMB. "I know it sounds cheesy but we do save lives," Ferguson told Ogazi. Like Ferguson, 30 percent of all nurses working in the United States have chosen to work in emergency nursing because they find the rewards so satisfying.

Nurses are responsible for administering tests and carrying out treatment prescribed by physicians as well as seeing to the well-being of their patients. But critically ill or injured patients need immediate, often specialized, care, and emergency nurses are trained to see to their needs as quickly as possible. Since these nurses are often the first to see patients when they arrive in the hospital, they must be able to rapidly diagnose a patient's condition, perform triage (which means prioritizing the order in which patients are treated), and immediately render lifesaving care. Depending upon their certifications, emergency nurses are trained to use complex medical equipment, perform tests, administer medication, and carry out other lifesaving procedures.

Despite their advanced skills, most of the time emergency nurses do not treat true emergencies. According to Olivet Nazarene University, only 13.3 percent of patients who come to the ER have medical problems that are serious enough to result in hospital admission. Some people come to the ER because they do not have health insurance or the funds to pay for their treatment, and ERs are often filled with people who simply need treatment for a minor medical problem. However, even in nonemergency situations, emergency nurses must treat each person with respect and provide the best care possible.

To be certified as an emergency nurse, registered nurses (RNs) must pass the Board Certified Emergency Nurse (BCEN) exam. It not necessary to be certified as an emergency nurse to work in emergency nursing; however, certification allows nurses to increase their knowledge base, secure better jobs, and increase their pay. RNs can also become certified in specific aspects of emergency nursing, such as pediatric emergencies, trauma, and emergency transport. Emergency pediatric nurses treat young children in emergency situations and often work at children's hospitals. Emergency trauma nurses deal with the types of injuries that can occur as a result of warfare, terrorist attacks, or natural disasters, and they usually work at trauma

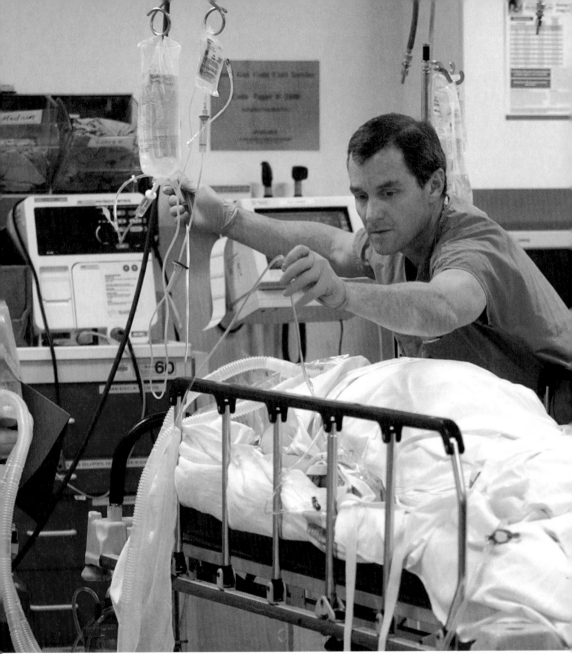

An nurse checks on a patient who was brought into a hospital emergency room. Emergency nursing is fast paced, chaotic, and exhausting but also extremely rewarding.

centers or pursue military careers. Emergency transport nurses specialize in critical care that must be given during ground or air transport and typically staff ambulances or medical transport airplanes and helicopters.

Some emergency nurses are also nurse practitioners. A nurse practitioner is a nurse with an advanced degree who is trained to work without the supervision of a physician. Emergency nurse practitioners can do many of the things that doctors do, such as ordering and interpreting X-rays and other tests, prescribing medication, and performing minor surgery. Although some emergency nurse practitioners work in settings alongside of physicians, most provide emergency care alone.

How Do You Become an Emergency Nurse?

Education

There are several routes to becoming a certified emergency nurse. After getting a high school diploma, students must complete a degree program in nursing and then become an RN. For their degree program, students can choose to earn either an associate of science degree in nursing or a bachelor of science degree in nursing from a university, accredited nursing school, or hospital. Nurses who want a career in the military can earn their degrees through a Reserve Officers' Training Corps, or ROTC, nursing program at a college or university.

After completing their degree program, students must pass the National Council Licensure Examination for Registered Nurses. Students who only have an associate's degree, which is typically a two-year degree, may have to take additional classes to pass the test; therefore, it is more common for those interested in emergency nursing to earn a bachelor's degree. Nurses who have these degrees also tend to earn higher pay and are promoted to positions of higher responsibility than those who have an associate's degree.

Another route to becoming an RN and pursuing emergency nursing is to first become a licensed practical nurse (LPN). To take the LPN exam, students only have to complete a one-year nursing program. LPNs are given less responsibility than RNs; they are not permitted to administer medication, supervise staff, or perform other advanced duties. The advantage to earning an LPN before pursing an RN is that LPNs can start working as nurses after just one year. In addition, some hospitals have tuition reimbursement programs that help LPNs continue their education and become RNs.

After becoming an RN, a nurse can work in an emergency room setting. To become certified in emergency nursing, an RN should have about two years of emergency nursing experience before taking the BCEN certification exam. There are many continuing education courses available to help nurses prepare for this exam. Certifications are also available in emergency pediatrics, emergency trauma, and emergency transport. All certified emergency nurses must be recertified every four years.

Volunteer Work and Internships

High school students who want to prepare for a career in nursing can volunteer at a hospital or an extended care facility. Volunteering can help students decide if nursing is the right career for them. Volunteering can also help a student get into a nursing program, and it is a great way to find a mentor or learn about scholarship opportunities. Hospitals that have their own nursing degree programs sometimes have volunteer programs designed to attract high school students who want to be nurses.

Hospital volunteers do not usually get to work in the emergency room, but an excellent way to get an idea of what emergency nursing entails is to volunteer at a local emergency medical services station or firehouse. Many of these stations have cadet programs for high school students who want to become emergency medical technicians (EMTs). Students can also become certified as EMTs once they are eighteen.

Skills and Personality

Emergency nurses do what they do because they get great satisfaction from saving lives. They have a passion for helping others and take great pride in their ability to do so on what is often the worst day of their patients' lives. They must be efficient, levelheaded, focused, and able to multitask. This type of nursing is not for everyone—there is no room for error in the emergency room, and those who do not thrive under stress may quickly become burned out.

Emergency nurses must also be compassionate. This is not always easy. Because people who visit the ER are usually under extreme stress, they can quickly become angry or even verbally abusive. In addition, because so many ER cases are not true emergencies, emergency nurses can feel frustrated that their skills are not being put to use. An ability to feel compassion for all people in distress is a critical trait of an emergency nurse.

Although it is important to be compassionate, nurses can be at risk of developing what is known as compassion fatigue. Compassion fatigue is a coping mechanism that may come into play when a nurse becomes emotionally exhausted from seeing too much pain and suffering. It is defined as an inability to feel compassion for a patient, which can affect one's ability to render the best care. Compassion fatigue can also impact a nurse's emotional life away from work. According to Olivet Nazarene University, 85 percent of emergency nurses experience at least one symptom of compassion fatigue during a typical week.

On the Job

Employers

Most emergency nurses are employed by hospital emergency rooms, trauma centers, and urgent care facilities. They can also be employed by organizations that provide health care at home to the elderly or disabled. Emergency transport or emergency trauma nurses often work for the military or for medical transport companies. Some emergency nurses work for governmental organizations or nonprofits that provide health care in remote areas where there is no access to emergency rooms or trauma centers.

Working Conditions

Emergency nurses work long hours. About 50 percent of all ER nurses work shifts longer than ten hours, and 40 percent work shifts longer than twelve hours. Work is fast paced, and nurses are usually on their feet for their entire shifts.

There are dangers to emergency nursing as well. Patients who have mental health issues or are under the influence of drugs or alcohol can quickly become erratic and attack their caregivers. Emergency rooms have procedures in place to protect nurses from such dangers, but verbal abuse is common and physical attacks do happen. According to Olivet Nazarene University, seven out of ten ER nurses have been verbally or physically assaulted while working. Nurses are also in danger of contracting diseases from their patients.

Earnings

In 2015 the pay range for RNs was $46,360 to $101,630 per year, with a median salary of $67,490, or $32.45 per hour. Pay range for nurse practitioners was $71,530 to $171,560 per year, with a median salary of $104,740, or $50.36 per hour. RNs and nurse practitioners working in emergency rooms or who have been certified in emergency nursing will tend to earn higher-than-average salaries. According to the website Nurse Journal, the average salary for all nurses who work in emergency rooms is $67,930.

Opportunities for Advancement

There are many opportunities for advancement for RNs who work in emergency nursing. An emergency nurse can move into a supervisory or administrative position, or he or she can earn an advanced degree and become a nurse practitioner or nursing instructor. In almost all cases, advancement and pay increases hinge upon continuing education and certification.

What Is the Future Outlook for Emergency Nurses?

According to Nurse Journal, emergency nursing will experience a 26 percent growth in employment through 2024—a growth rate that is much faster than the national average. This is because the aging population is increasing, which means there will be more age-related emergencies coming into emergency rooms across the country. Nurses who wish to specialize in emergency nursing will have excellent career prospects in the coming decade.

Find Out More

American Association of Critical-Care Nurses (AACN)
101 Columbia
Aliso Viejo, CA 92656
website: www.aacn.org

The AACN is the largest advocacy organization for emergency and critical care nurses in the world. Its website has information about education, training, and certification; issues relating to what emergency nurses do; and links to various publications, including career bulletins.

Emergency Nurses Association (ENA)
915 Lee St.
Des Plaines, IL 60016
website: www.ena.org

The ENA is an education and advocacy organization dedicated to supporting emergency nursing professionals. Its website includes information about emergency nursing certifications, practice and research in the field, career opportunities, and links to various ENA publications.

EveryNurse.org
2926 Juniper St.
San Diego, CA 92104
website: www.everynurse.org

EveryNurse.org is a nursing career research website that includes career descriptions, interviews, licensing information, and employer profiles. It contains a section devoted to emergency nursing that includes day-in-the-life videos and details about specific educational and licensing requirements.

Society of Trauma Nurses (STN)
446 E. High St., Suite 10
Lexington, KY 40507
website: www.traumanurses.org

The STN is a professional organization devoted to improving the quality of trauma care through education and advocacy of emergency, critical care, and trauma nurses. Its website has educational and career information as well as links to emergency nursing publications and a resource library.

Search and Rescue Specialist

A hiker is trapped on a mountain summit, a building collapses, a hurricane hits, a plane crashes in the ocean, a child disappears in a state park—these are the situations in which search and rescue (SAR) specialists go into action.

Search and rescue is divided into five broad areas: urban SAR, ground SAR, mountain rescue, air-sea rescue, and combat SAR (also known as pararescue). Urban SAR teams are deployed when disaster strikes a city or other heavily populated area. These specialists know how to search unstable or collapsed buildings, how to avoid the dangers posed by downed electrical wires or broken gas lines, and how to rescue people with traumatic injuries. Urban SAR specializes in large-scale disasters with multiple victims. In contrast, ground SAR is usually deployed when a person or small

At a Glance:
Search and Rescue Specialist

Minimum Educational Requirements
Bachelor's degree

Personal Qualities
High stress tolerance; team player; compassion

Certifications
Required

Working Conditions
Indoors and outdoors; high risk of injury

Salary Range
About $26,000 to $146,000

Future Job Outlook
Specific numbers are unavailable

aircraft is missing and a large area must be searched—even if that area is a city. These specialists have expert knowledge in ground and air search techniques and understand how lost people typically behave. For instance, according to Paul, a Sierra wilderness ground SAR team captain, "Sixty percent of hunters follow water. Berry pickers go uphill." As he explains to Lauren Sheppard of Salary.com, "Someone who is trained [in wilderness survival] might build a shelter, forage for food, or try to build a fire. Someone who's not will seek natural shelter in caves, and more often than not end up in a mountain lion's den or an old mine shaft."

Mountain rescue is a highly specialized area of SAR. Mountain SAR specialists are expert climbers who have advanced wilderness skills. They rescue people who are trapped in the mountains or in other remote areas that are impossible to reach with conventional vehicles. Air-sea rescue is deployed when watercraft is lost at sea or people fall overboard. These specialists search by plane and perform water rescues. Finally, combat rescue is carried out by the military when soldiers are trapped in combat zones. Also, any area of SAR might use highly trained search dogs to help with a search mission. Dogs can be trained to locate victims under debris or to track a person's scent through the wilderness. Search and rescue specialists who use dogs are called K9 SAR handlers.

Search and rescue is primarily a volunteer endeavor; however, specialists at the top of their fields can become members of elite SAR units. Urban SAR specialists and K9 SAR handlers can join one of the twenty-eight urban SAR task forces of the Federal Emergency Management Agency (FEMA), which have been deployed in disasters such as the World Trade Center bombings and Hurricane Katrina. Mountain SAR specialists can join the Yosemite Search and Rescue team, a group of elite climbers who rescue people lost or injured in Yosemite National Park. All of these elite specialists are passionate about search and rescue and go through rigorous, time-consuming, and expensive training and certification programs. They must be ready to deploy to a disaster site at a moment's notice and can spend weeks on a SAR mission. However, they are only paid during deployment and appointments usually last only two years, so most have second careers. For instance, mountain SAR specialists may also be park rangers, urban SAR specialists may be firefighters or nurses, and K9 SAR handlers may be professional dog trainers. Many SAR specialists also have careers in the military—particularly in the US Coast Guard, which handles many air-sea rescues.

Those interested in pursuing a full-time career in search and rescue will probably not be able to find a paid position right out of college. Because most full-time jobs are highly specialized, they are usually reserved for people who already have extensive experience. Most involve managing programs within FEMA, but highly experienced individuals can also find positions managing state SAR programs or teaching SAR techniques. For instance, urban SAR specialists who also have program management expertise can find positions overseeing state or city urban SAR programs. These specialists supervise volunteer teams, evaluate emergency procedures, develop and deliver training, and take care of associated administrative duties. Skilled K9 SAR trainers can work for organizations that specialize in training search dogs. Finally, some SAR experts have started private companies. For instance, SAR specialist Harry Oakes started International K9 Search and Rescue Services in Longview, Washington, as a way to offer search and rescue services to private citizens. His company helps families find their lost loved ones and pets and averages 750 SAR missions a year.

Because it might be difficult to find a full-time job in SAR, most experts say that only those who have a true passion for the work should specialize in this area of emergency response. Those who do often get great satisfaction from using their expertise—whether that be in emergency medicine, mountain climbing, dog training, or piloting aircraft—to save lives. Oakes does not regret a moment of his forty-four years of involvement in SAR—even though it has left him with permanent lung damage from crawling through collapsed buildings to search for survivors. "Was it worth it? Sure I would do it all over again," he writes in a personal e-mail. "I've done over eleven thousand, nine hundred and sixty SAR calls over the years and saved quite a few people, young and old." For specialists like Oakes, SAR is more than a career; it is a calling.

How Do You Become a Search and Rescue Specialist?

Education

There are no formal educational requirements to volunteer in search and rescue, but students who are considering a career in this area will need a four-year college degree. What a student chooses as a major really depends upon his or her interests. For instance, those interested in managing urban SAR programs should pursue a degree in public or business administration and then get practical experience managing governmental programs. Those interested in mountain rescue should become park rangers, and they will need a degree in an area like wildlife and forestry, park and restoration management, or environmental studies. Those who want to teach search and rescue might pursue a degree in education with a focus on adult education or instructional design. And students interested in air or water rescue will find the best career prospects in the military, which offers training and other educational opportunities.

Continuing education and certifications in areas specific to one's specialty—such as fire technology, hazardous material response, emergency medical services, or K9 SAR handling—will also be important to securing a full time job. There are countless training opportunities offered all over the country, many of which offer formal certifications.

While in high school, students can start learning about their area of interest, whether that is wilderness survival, rock climbing, dog training, or emergency medicine. In addition, all students contemplating this career—or any career in emergency response—should get certified in CPR and first aid.

Volunteer Work and Internships

Volunteering is key to pursuing a career in search and rescue, and students should start volunteering as soon as possible. One excellent way to gain experience is by joining the Civil Air Patrol (CAP), an auxiliary of the US Air Force that trains young people in ground and air SAR techniques and assists in ground searches for people and aircraft.

A man who collapsed in a remote mountain area is carried by search and rescue specialists to a waiting helicopter. These specialists are trained to search different environments including collapsed buildings, mountains, and oceans for lost and injured people.

Most areas have a local CAP cadet squadron, which is open to young people aged twelve to nineteen. Students can also check the age requirements of their local search and rescue organizations. Most states have many such organizations. For instance, the Virginia Search and Rescue Council lists twenty-two volunteer SAR organizations on its website, including seven organizations that specialize in K9 SAR and fourteen that specialize in ground search.

Skills and Personality

When disaster strikes, SAR specialists are willing to put aside all other obligations to help those in need. They are levelheaded in an emergency, are both leaders and team players, and love to learn and are constantly improving their skills. Like emergency medical technicians and firefighters, they thrive under pressure and can endure stress, frustration, and physical hardship. However, emergencies do not happen every day—or even every month—and those who pursue a full-time career in SAR must be willing to spend much of their time on nonemergency tasks. For instance, program directors do mostly administrative work, and park rangers spend a lot of their time educating the public.

When there is a disaster, the emotional effects on the rescuers can be profound. Victims are not always found alive, or found at all, and victims' bodies can be badly damaged. Because of this, some specialists burn out after a few years and others suffer from post-traumatic stress disorder. Those considering a career in SAR should be prepared to experience some emotional trauma.

On the Job

Employers

The largest employers of SAR specialists are the US military and FEMA, but paid positions are also available in state and city governments. Some police and fire departments in large urban areas also have SAR positions available within their emergency management departments. The National Park Service also employs SAR specialists, as do a few nonprofit and private companies.

Working Conditions

Search and rescue is extremely hazardous. Searchers can be subjected to dangerous surroundings and extreme weather. Urban SAR specialists can be crushed by collapsing buildings and injured by toxins and debris. And both ground and mountain specialists are exposed to treacherous wilderness terrain.

Time is of the essence in SAR, and searchers often work around the clock in emergencies. Between emergencies, career SAR specialists usually work full-time jobs in an office or teaching environment.

Earnings

Because full-time positions are so varied, SAR specialists earn a wide range of salaries. FEMA task force members are paid an hourly rate while on a mission, which varies based on their position. For instance, a K9 handler can earn up to $28 an hour and a trauma surgeon can earn up to $52 an hour. Salaries for full-time specialists range from about $26,000 for dog trainers to about $146,000 for FEMA program managers. According to Indeed.com, park rangers make an average of $33,000 and urban SAR specialists make an average of $43,000.

Opportunities for Advancement

There are fewer than ten thousand paid positions in SAR nationally. Those jobs are the advanced positions in SAR, so once a specialist secures a paid position, there may be no way to advance further—at least in pay and responsibilities. However, there is always room to advance one's knowledge and skills.

What Is the Future Outlook for Search and Rescue Specialists?

There is no official data available about the employment outlook for SAR specialists. Most jobs are with government agencies or with nonprofit organizations, which rely on tax dollars or donations. Even though many localities are facing budget cuts, it is likely that recent increases in extreme weather and terrorist activities will create a need for more SAR specialists. And there will always be a need for compassionate, well-trained people to come to the aid of those who need rescue.

Find Out More

Civil Air Patrol (CAP)
CAP National Headquarters
105 S. Hansell St., Bldg. 714
Maxwell Air Force Base, AL 36112
website: www.gocivilairpatrol.com

As the US Air Force's civilian auxiliary, CAP's mission includes training adults and young people in ground and air SAR techniques and mobilizing them in SAR emergencies. Its website contains details and news about the organization and information about local CAP squadrons and how to volunteer.

Friends of Yosemite Search and Rescue (YOSAR)
PO Box 611
Yosemite, CA 95389
website: www.friendsofyosar.org

Friends of YOSAR is a nonprofit organization that supports YOSAR, the emergency response team for Yosemite National Park. Its website contains information about YOSAR teams and what they do, including their helicopter rescue program and their K9 SAR program. Information about past rescues and various mountain rescue techniques are also provided.

National Association for Search and Rescue (NASAR)
PO Box 232020
Centreville, VA 20120
website: www.nasar.org

NASAR is an educational and credentialing organization that trains professionals and volunteers in SAR techniques and management. Its website contains information about courses and training as well as links to blogs and newsletters written about SAR techniques.

Search Dog Foundation (SDF)
501 E. Ojai Ave.
Ojai, CA 93023
website: www.searchdogfoundation.org

The SDF is the preeminent search dog-training organization in the United States. Its mission is to partner rescued dogs with first responders and train both at no cost to find people buried alive in the wreckage of disasters. Its website contains information about K9 SAR and various SDF deployments, as well as links to articles of interest to those interested in K9 SAR handling.

US SAR Task Force (USSARTF)
PO Box 11292
Elkins Park, PA 19027
website: www.ussartf.org

The USSARTF is a nonprofit organization of SAR specialists operating primarily in the Northeast. It mobilizes during SAR emergencies, conducts training and certification, and consults with government agencies about SAR and disaster relief programs and planning. Its website contains information about various volunteer SAR training and certification programs. It also includes reference materials about all facets of SAR, including wilderness survival, hypothermia, and map basics.

Emergency Management Specialist

At a Glance:
Emergency Management Specialist

Minimum Educational Requirements
Bachelor's degree or equivalent

Personal Qualities
Excellent interpersonal, decision-making, critical-thinking, and leadership skills

Certification
Required in some states

Working Conditions
Primarily indoors

Salary Range
About $34,000 to $127,180

Number of Jobs
As of 2014 about 10,500

Future Job Outlook
Growth rate of 6 percent through 2024

What Does an Emergency Management Specialist Do?

Emergency management specialists prepare their communities or organizations for disasters like earthquakes, hurricanes, floods, industrial accidents, or terrorist attacks. Their goal is to create plans that will decrease the effects of these disasters. In private companies, this may mean ensuring the safety of employees and minimizing the effect of the disaster on production (this is often called business continuity planning). In communities, this may mean deploying first responders, putting evacuation plans in place, making sure hospitals are prepared to treat an influx of injured people and that lines of communication remain open, restoring utilities and making sure those without power or clean water are cared for, and cleaning up after the disaster. In addition, many specialists work with other areas of public safety to reduce the risk of emergencies occurring. For instance, specialists may become involved in efforts to build flood walls in areas prone to flooding or may recommend emergency shutoff valves be installed on gas lines in areas prone to earthquakes. They also make sure everyone involved in emergency response is properly trained to carry out emergency response plans, and they frequently test those plans and monitor performance.

During disasters, emergency management specialists use a management tool called the incident command system (ICS), which was first developed in the 1970s to manage large-scale responses to wildfires in California and Arizona. The ICS defines the broad scope of responsibilities for all groups involved in emergency response and establishes a chain of command so that organizations can work together quickly and efficiently. The system can be adapted for use in small-scale emergencies like traffic accidents and large-scale disasters like earthquakes or floods. Specialists also work to adapt and expand the ICS into specific plans for the types of disasters that may affect their organizations, and they must be thoroughly familiar with the ICS framework and planning capabilities. The ICS has also been used as a framework for developing various computer programs that specialists use for communication and managing resources. Specialists must be well versed in the ICS and any related computer systems used in their organization.

On a day-to-day basis, specialists tend to spend their time working with various organizations to put emergency plans in place and make sure they work effectively. They do research, review regulations, lead training sessions, and oversee public education on emergency preparedness. Between emergencies, their jobs may seem somewhat dull and routine. But when disaster strikes, they must respond immediately and coordinate all aspects of response and recovery, making decisions and staying calm under extreme stress. This highly competitive career is not for everyone, but those who do it well are responsible for making emergency response happen.

How Do You Become an Emergency Management Specialist?

Education

In almost all cases, emergency management specialists must have a bachelor's degree in business or public administration, accounting, finance, public health, emergency management, or a related field. Some businesses concerned with protecting their computer systems during an emergency require a degree in computer science or information systems administration. Some large organizations require applicants to have a master's degree. Many organizations require their specialists to hold a certification in emergency management, either before or shortly after they are hired. Certifications can be obtained from the International Association of Emergency Managers in Falls Church, Virginia, or the Disaster Recovery Institute International in New York City.

Volunteer Work and Internships

Emergency management specialists must have more than strong management skills; they must have advanced knowledge of all facets of disaster response. They also must have experience in disaster management and be able to demonstrate that they can work well under stress. Most gain these skills and experience by volunteering in emergency response. Some may be involved in their local search and rescue group and act as volunteer directors during an emergency. Others may be volunteer firefighters and have advanced education and certifications in fire technology or emergency medical services. Students interested in a career in emergency management should become as active as possible in volunteer emergency response while in high school and college. Internships in emergency management are also available for college students in organizations like the Federal Emergency Management Association (FEMA).

Having these experiences on one's résumé greatly increases the chance of getting a job in emergency management. For instance, Janusz Wasiolek was encouraged to pursue a career in emergency management by his supervisor while volunteering for the Illinois Medical

Emergency Response Team (IMERT). He eventually enrolled in a graduate program in emergency management and got a job with the National Association of County and City Health Officials Public Health Preparedness Team. "The reason I was hired," he writes in a June 2011 article for the online magazine *Emergency Management*, "was not because I was enrolled in George Washington University's program, but rather my past involvement with IMERT and experience as a paramedic."

Skills and Personality

Emergency management specialists are primarily managers. To be able to manage people and resources in a crisis, one must have strong leadership skills. Not everyone has the skills and personality to lead. Strong leaders are not just decisive, critical thinkers; they listen to those who report to them and defer to their expertise when appropriate. Their knowledge is often broad rather than deep, and they are good at delegating responsibility and empowering those under them. When things go well, they give credit to others; when mistakes are made, they take responsibility. Those who enjoy developing expertise in a subject, prefer to do things themselves rather than delegate, and enjoy helping people directly should probably avoid a career in emergency management.

The day-to-day work of an emergency management specialist is similar to that of any program manager. They are involved in the bureaucratic work of managing resources and funding, designing and evaluating systems, ensuring compliance with regulations, and doing routine office tasks. They must understand how large, complex systems work and be able to anticipate the problems that might occur. They must be good communicators and collaborators. Finally, they must have strong people skills so that they can forge relationships with other organizations.

On the Job

Employers

The US Bureau of Labor Statistics (BLS) has changed the name of this occupation from *emergency management specialist* to *emergency management director*, but the term *specialist* is still used by most employers. According to the BLS, more than half of these professionals are employed by local, state, and federal governments. The rest are employed by hospitals; colleges, universities, and professional schools; and private companies like power and chemical plants, pharmaceutical companies, and companies that provide contracting services to the government. For instance, the management company Booz Allen Hamilton employs emergency management specialists to provide disaster planning and management services to various governmental agencies.

Working Conditions

Most of the time, emergency management specialists work in an office environment and keep typical office hours. However, they must be on call at all times. During emergencies, these specialists must work long hours and be available around the clock. Many specialists must also spend time at disaster sites to direct and evaluate disaster response. In addition, specialists usually must travel a great deal to meet with government agencies and community groups. They also frequently attend conferences and training sessions around the country.

During an emergency, specialists are under a tremendous amount of stress. They must make critical decisions such as how and when to order evacuations and how to best manage the logistics of deploying various first responders. Lives depend on these decisions, and their every move is often scrutinized by governmental agencies and the media. An ability to lead under stress is critical to success in this profession.

Earnings

According to the BLS, in 2015 the pay range for an emergency management director (or specialist) was $34,000 to $127,180 per year, with a median salary of $67,330. The highest-paid emergency management specialists work for colleges, universities, and professional schools and make an average of $86,500. The lowest-paid specialists work in state government (not including state colleges and hospitals) and make an average of $58,600.

Opportunities for Advancement

Emergency management specialists who are in charge of their organization's emergency management program usually cannot advance any further within that organization. However, specialists can take on more responsibility and earn more pay by seeking out positions within larger organizations like universities, city or state governments, or FEMA. Competition for these jobs is strong, and those hired must have a great deal of disaster management experience.

It is important to note that the more responsibility one is given, the less work he or she will do on the ground during a disaster. High-level emergency management specialists are in charge of multiple emergency response programs and direct the overall response to large-scale disasters; therefore, they rarely work directly with first responder groups on the ground. Because of this, many specialists prefer to work within smaller organizations.

What Is the Future Outlook for Emergency Management Specialists?

Although there will always be a need for emergency response, many people believe there will be an increase in natural and man-made disasters over the next decade. Most experts say that coastal areas will see more instances of flooding and storm damage due to global warming. In addition, the increase in terrorist activity and mass shootings also shows no signs of declining. Since the national disasters caused by Hurricane Katrina and by the terrorist attacks on the World Trade Center, there has been an increase in the emphasis placed on disaster planning. For this reason, it is likely that the need for emergency management specialists will increase over the next decade as more and more local governments, hospitals, school districts, and large companies plan how to keep people safe and stay operational during an emergency.

However, because of the general downturn in the economy in recent years, many localities are facing budget cuts. For this reason, the BLS projects only an average growth rate of about 6 percent in new jobs created in this field over the next decade. Because there are only about ten thousand emergency management positions in the country, this small increase in growth will not result in many more jobs being created. Larger private companies will probably see the most growth, as will emergency management consulting companies. Smaller organizations that cannot afford to create full-time emergency management positions may instead hire consultants or simply develop their own plans in-house.

This all may change, however, if the country faces another large-scale disaster or terrorist attack. Then, the public will most likely demand that more money is allocated to emergency planning, which will in turn create more jobs in all areas of emergency response, including emergency management.

Find Out More

Emergency Management
100 Blue Ravine Rd.
Folsom, CA 95630
website: www.emergencymgmt.com

Emergency Management is an award-winning online magazine that covers issues that pertain to emergency management, public safety, and homeland security professionals. Its website contains in-depth articles, links to blogs relating to emergency management, and a jobs section.

GovernmentJobs.com
website: www.governmentjobs.com

The emergency management section of the website GovernmentJobs.com contains a roundup of available positions and internships in emergency management around the country. Each job description includes a salary range and detailed information about job scope and necessary qualifications. This site can give students a good idea of what is required of emergency management specialists in various positions and what opportunities are available.

International Association of Emergency Managers (IAEM)
201 Park Washington Ct.
Falls Church, VA 22046
website: www.iaem.com

The IAEM is an international nonprofit organization dedicated to promoting the principles of emergency management and representing emergency management professionals. Its website contains information about the principles and ethics of emergency management, articles and newsletters aimed at emergency management professionals, and listings of jobs and internships.

National Emergency Management Association (NEMA)
1776 Avenue of the States
Lexington, KY 40511
website: www.nemaweb.org

NEMA is a national professional organization of emergency management specialists. Its website has information about careers in emergency management as well as a library that includes information about national issues in emergency management, state agencies, homeland security, and about webinars that discuss working as an emergency management specialist.

Trauma Surgeon

What Does a Trauma Surgeon Do?

On January 8, 2011, twenty-two-year-old Jared Lee Loughner opened fire on a crowd outside of a shopping center in Tucson, Arizona, where US representative Gabrielle Giffords was giving a speech. Loughner shot nineteen people, including Giffords and nine-year-old Christina Taylor-Green. Giffords and Taylor-Green were taken to the trauma center at University Medical Center Tucson (UMCT), where Giffords, who had been shot through the head, was rushed into surgery. Taylor-Green, whose heart had stopped, had been receiving CPR for more than twenty minutes when she arrived. Protocol dictated that Taylor-Green should be pronounced dead, but in a last-ditch effort to save her life, trauma surgeon Randall Friese opened her chest, inserted a tube to fill her heart with blood, and massaged her heart with his hand. Even though it took less than two minutes for Friese to begin the open heart massage, he could not restart the little girl's heart. Giffords was miraculously saved by the

---

At a Glance:
Trauma Surgeon

Minimum Educational Requirements
Doctor of medicine degree, five-year residency, one- to two-year fellowship

Personal Qualities
Complex problem-solving and decision-making skills; high stress tolerance; manual dexterity

Certification
Required

Working Conditions
Indoors

Salary Range
About $277,432 to $501,963

Number of Jobs
As of 2015 fewer than 5,990

Future Job Outlook
Growth rate of at least 14 percent through 2024

trauma team, but Taylor-Green's injuries were simply too extensive.

Trauma surgeons like those staffing UMCT's trauma center are trained to perform emergency surgical procedures to treat traumatic injuries, including fractures, cuts, blunt force trauma, burns, gunshot and stabbing wounds, and damage caused by explosions. A patient who has undergone trauma—for instance, the victim of a car crash—often has multiple internal and external injuries that must be assessed. When a trauma victim arrives at an emergency room or trauma center, a trauma surgeon usually takes charge of the patient as soon as possible. He or she must rapidly evaluate the patient's injuries, order whatever diagnostic tests are needed, and either perform surgery or call in another surgical specialist, such as a neurosurgeon. Unlike emergency room physicians, who only provide care in the emergency room, trauma surgeons are also responsible for caring for the patient after surgery.

Trauma surgeons specialize in surgery of the neck, chest, abdomen, and extremities. They are also trained in nonsurgical critical care procedures. In the United States, trauma surgeons typically call in specialists to perform surgery on the brain, the face, and the musculoskeletal system. When multiple surgeries are needed, trauma surgeons may work alongside of these specialists in the operating room.

How Do You Become a Trauma Surgeon?

Education

Becoming a trauma surgeon is a huge commitment. These surgeons must accumulate about fifteen years of higher education and training before they are board certified in trauma surgery. Those interested in this career should start preparing in high school. Students should focus on math and science and get a strong foundation in biology, chemistry, and physics. How a student performs in these classes is a good indication of whether he or she should become a physician.

Students will first need to earn a bachelor of science degree and do well enough to be accepted to medical school. Some undergraduate programs have a track of premedical, or premed, studies—a series of required courses that helps prepare the student for medical school. Students who choose a premed track will still have to choose their major, which can be in biology, chemistry or organic chemistry, physics, or another scientific field. Getting good grades is crucial to being accepted to medical school, which is a four-year graduate program that awards a doctor of medicine degree upon graduation.

To apply to medical school, students must pass the Medical School Admission Test (MCAT), a standardized test frequently taken in the third year of undergraduate studies. Strong performance on the MCAT, good grades, and a demonstrated commitment to medicine through extracurricular studies are determining factors in whether or not a student is accepted. Some medical schools will accept a student after only three years of undergraduate work.

Students in medical school typically spend their first two years studying in a classroom setting and the second two years getting experience in a hospital setting under the supervision of a physician. Before entering their third year of medical school, students must pass the first part of the US Medical Licensing Examination (USMLE). During their fourth year, they must pass the second part of the USMLE. They also apply for a residency program—an in-depth training program—in their chosen specialty during the fourth year.

Residency programs are very competitive, and not all of those applying for a surgical residency will be chosen. Those who are will spend a minimum of five years as an apprentice surgeon and will learn surgical and clinical practices at a teaching hospital. After their first year, residents usually take the third part of the USMLE. In their later years of the program, residents perform surgery under close supervision.

Trauma surgery is a surgical specialty that requires two additional years of study, which is called a fellowship. Fellows usually work in a trauma center learning specialized techniques in trauma surgery and acute care. They must take several certifying examinations, including exams in general surgery and surgical critical care. Fellows are also sometimes required to teach residents.

After completing their fellowships and passing all required examinations, trauma surgeons typically seek out positions in the emergency medical divisions of hospitals.

Volunteer Work and Internships

Students interested in trauma surgery should volunteer as emergency medical technicians (EMTs). EMTs must be at least eighteen years old and go through a training and certification program, but teens may be able to volunteer in a program designed for high school students. Working as an EMT in high school and college will help with acceptance to medical school. It will also give students an excellent perspective on what it is like to deal with traumatic injuries.

In addition, many teaching hospitals have programs that allow students to observe operations, shadow surgeons and other emergency medical professionals, and gain experience in the emergency room.

Skills and Personality

A trauma surgeon is the physician in charge when someone has been critically injured; therefore, he or she must be a natural leader who is comfortable being in charge of others—including other physicians. This takes confidence and self-assurance, but it also takes humility and the ability to recognize when another surgical specialist is needed. Trauma surgeons must also be critical thinkers who can make quick decisions under extreme stress. Because these surgeons usually see their patients in the emergency room, they must bring all of their expertise into play while their patients are in critical condition (and possibly conscious and in great pain). This takes a cool head; trauma surgeons must thrive under pressure and must have laser focus in the midst of chaos.

All surgeons, including trauma surgeons, have the reputation of lacking compassion for their patients. Although almost everyone who pursues a career in medicine is motivated by a desire to help others, there is a reason that trauma surgeons may seem unfeeling at times. Quick thinking and decisive action often means the difference between life and death, and surgeons cannot afford to become distracted by their emotions. Empathy—the ability to feel what others feel—must be switched off in an emergency. In fact, brain studies have shown that even the most compassionate health care providers have learned how to switch off their empathy so that they can provide the best care. This does not mean that trauma surgeons do not care about their patients; for instance, caring about the life of Christina Taylor-Green is what motivated Dr. Friese to take such extraordinary measures to try to save her. But it is important to understand that managing one's emotions is necessary in this profession. Not everyone can do this, and it is not uncommon for students to discover in medical school that their personalities are simply not suited for a career as a surgeon.

Employers

Trauma surgeons are employed by hospitals and work within a hospital's emergency room or trauma center. They can also work in teaching hospitals that offer fellowships in trauma or acute care surgery. Trauma surgeons are also employed by the military, where they may work in combat conditions to treat battlefield injuries.

Working Conditions

Trauma surgeons work long hours and have difficulty finding a work-life balance. Other types of surgeons generally have medical practices outside of the hospital and schedule surgery during normal working hours. Trauma surgeons, however, must be physically at the trauma center—or on call nearby—so that they can perform surgery at a moment's notice. In emergencies, they may be up for days at a time, performing complex surgeries and overseeing their patients' recoveries. And because there is a shortage of trauma surgeons nationwide, they are often overloaded with patients, especially during disasters. Because of this, many trauma surgeons experience burnout—a psychological condition characterized by a lack of motivation, exhaustion, and frustration. In fact, a 2015 survey by the American College of Surgeons found that being a trauma surgeon was the number-one factor associated with burnout among surgeons.

However, some people find the life of a trauma surgeon exhilarating. More than any other profession in emergency response, trauma surgeons are the most qualified to save lives. Those suited for the demands of this profession find this career to be extremely rewarding.

Earnings

Surgeons are among the highest-paid professionals in all professions. According to Salary.com, the pay range for trauma surgeons is $277,432 to $501,963 per year, with a median salary of $369,559 as of 2016. According to the Medical Group Management Association, the average salary of a trauma surgeon is about $432,000 per year.

Opportunities for Advancement

Trauma surgeons can increase their salary by increasing their skills, their experience, and their standing within their field. Those with the most experience often lead—or even create—specialized trauma centers or teach trauma surgical techniques at teaching hospitals. However, some trauma surgeons become burned out by this highly stressful profession and shift their surgical specialty. Surgeons who specialize in neurology, cardiology, and orthopedics all earn more than trauma surgeons and have a much more satisfying work-life balance.

What Is the Future Outlook for Trauma Surgeons?

According to reports from the American College of Surgeons' National Trauma Data Bank, the number of traumatic injuries in the United States is on the rise, from 681,000 incidents in 2010 to 860,000 in 2014. To meet this demand, more and more hospitals are building trauma and critical care centers. The US Bureau of Labor Statistics (BLS) projects that the growth rate among all physicians and surgeons is much faster than average at 14 percent over the next decade.

There has been a shortage of both emergency physicians and trauma surgeons in the United States for many years—in part because these specialists work long hours and are at high risk for malpractice lawsuits. There are not enough trauma surgeons practicing today to staff trauma centers and emergency rooms, and there are not enough doctors pursuing careers in trauma surgery to meet the future demand. The BLS notes that, as of 2015, there were only 5,990 surgeons employed directly by general medical and surgical hospitals (these are the surgeons most likely to be performing trauma surgery). Because of this shortage, those who choose a career in trauma surgery will have no difficulty finding a job at a trauma center or emergency room in the decade to come.

Find Out More

American Association for the Surgery of Trauma (AAST)
633 N. Saint Clair St., Suite 2600
Chicago, IL 60611
website: www.aast.org

The AAST is an association of trauma surgeons and other acute care professionals dedicated to the advancement of knowledge in treating and preventing traumatic injuries. Its website contains information about various types of traumatic injuries, career and scholarship information, and links to various newsletters and publications, including the *Journal of Traumatic & Acute Care Surgery.*

American College of Surgeons (ACS)
633 N. Saint Clair St.
Chicago, IL 60611
website: www.facs.org

The ACS is an association of surgeons dedicated to improving surgical care through education and research. The trauma program section of its website has information about trauma as a surgical specialty, trauma education and injury prevention, and an archive of trauma-related newsletters and other publications.

National Association of EMS Physicians (NAEMSP)
PO Box 19570
Lenexa, KS 66285
website: www.naemsp.org

The NAEMSP is an association of emergency medical services physicians, trauma surgeons, and other critical care professionals who serve as a resource to their peers. Its website includes information about trauma surgery as a surgical subspecialty, forums, and links to newsletters and publications.

Trauma Center Association of America (TCAA)
650 Montana Ave., Suite A
Las Cruces, NM 88001
website: www.traumacenters.org

The TCAA's mission is to assist and support trauma centers with policy development, operations, and financial management. Its website contains information about trauma centers in the news, publications and newsletters, and careers for surgeons and other trauma center professionals.

Interview with a Firefighter

Michael Crumbaker is a career firefighter with twenty-six years of experience at the Anne Arundel County Fire Department in Millersville, Maryland. He started volunteering at the department when he was sixteen, began driving emergency vehicles at seventeen, was certified as an emergency medical technician (EMT) at eighteen, and was hired as a firefighter and EMT just after his twentieth birthday. He answered questions about his career by e-mail.

Q: Why did you become a firefighter?

A: My grandfather was a firefighter and one of the first ambulance drivers in his region. I grew up with a fire radio scanner nearby and sometimes went on late night trips to big fires in Baltimore. Then in 1987, when I was in the tenth grade, the worst (at the time) train collision in Amtrak history occurred a block from my home. This incident affected my community for weeks and had a huge impact on me. I immersed myself in emergency services classes or ambulance driving during the day and lived in a volunteer firehouse at night while I applied for a job at every fire department in the area.

Q: Can you describe your typical workday?

A: My workday usually begins at 7 a.m. and ends around 7 a.m. the next day, though forty-eight-hour shifts are not unusual. A shift begins with checking over the equipment and vehicles. Days are spent maintaining the fire station and its records; inspecting nearby businesses, apartment buildings, and government buildings; training; and conducting public education events. Meals are usually eaten at the fire station. We all understand that our work will be frequently interrupted by emergency calls. At night, if there are no calls for help, we may even get to sleep.

Q: What do you like most and least about your job?

A: The best part of this job is something I carry with me on or off duty and will take with me when I retire. That is the knowledge that when something goes wrong, I know how to help fix it. This brings me a sense of peace that outweighs what is for many the worst part of the job: seeing terrible things happen to people. Also, because we share these experiences, there is camaraderie among firefighters that you don't get with most other careers.

My least favorite part of this business is the politics and resistance to change. Every fire station is different and has its own rules and procedures, and every one is certain its way is the one true way.

Q: What personal qualities do you find most valuable for this type of work?

A: The personal qualities needed for this job include the ability to change roles quickly. During one part of the day, I might be in charge of a five-person crew operating millions of dollars' worth of equipment while news helicopters film our response to an emergency. Next I'll be cleaning the toilet and mopping the floor. Later I'll be driving a homeless person to the hospital. Tonight I'll calculate the approximate amount of water needed to extinguish a fire that has consumed 50 percent of the McDonald's that just opened, but not before I clean the blood and vomit off my boots.

Of course you have to want to help other people, but you also have to be able to handle them during the worst day of their lives. You have to shrug off criticism and anger and just smile and do your job, even when you are helping someone who doesn't really need the help.

Q: What advice do you have for students who might be interested in this career?

A: Firefighting is a very competitive field—the typical hiring process starts with over a thousand applicants for fifty positions, and the selection process can take six months or more. You should start preparing for this career well before adulthood, like I did, and volunteer in your teens. A solid performance in high school and being physically fit are very important, as is driving experience with a clean driving record. A good reputation with other employers is important, and don't forget about those drug tests. EMT classes are desirable and sometimes required. Fire science or management classes are unlikely to help you get hired, but they will come in to play when it is time for promotions. Most fire departments prefer to train their own people because, remember, they think their way of teaching is the best. Volunteer experience and military service can also be helpful.

Other Jobs in Emergency Response

Aviation rescue swimmer
Critical care nurse
Director of emergency services
Disaster program specialist
Disaster workforce coordinator
Emergency logistics coordinator
Emergency management
  program assistant
Emergency management
  training coordinator
Emergency physician assistant
Emergency planning manager
Emergency room physician
Emergency services counselor
EMS coordinator
EMS pilot
EMT ambulance driver

EMT/paramedic instructor
Fire technology instructor
Hazardous materials removal
  specialist
K9 SAR handler
Lifeguard
Pararescue specialist
Park ranger
Safety officer
Search and rescue pilot
Search dog trainer
Ski patrol team member
Smoke jumper (Firefighter)
SWAT team member
Swift water rescue specialist
Wildland firefighter

Editor's Note: The US Department of Labor's Bureau of Labor Statistics provides information about hundreds of occupations. The agency's *Occupational Outlook Handbook* describes what these jobs entail, the work environment, education and skill requirements, pay, future outlook, and more. The *Occupational Outlook Handbook* may be accessed online at www.bls.gov/ooh.

Index

Note: Boldface page numbers indicate illustrations

About the Author

Christine Wilcox writes fiction and nonfiction for young adults and adults. She has worked as an editor, an instructional designer, and a writing instructor. She lives in Richmond, Virginia, with her husband, David, and her son, Doug.